D1389058

MARKS &
SPENCER

# fish &
# seafood

simple and delicious easy-to-make recipes

June Hammond

Marks and Spencer p.l.c.
Baker Street, London, W1U 8EP

www.marksandspencer.com

Copyright © Exclusive Editions 2002

All rights reserved. No part of this publication
may be reproduced, stored in a retrieval system or
transmitted, in any form or by any means, electronic,
mechanical, photocopying, recording or otherwise,
without the prior permission of the copyright holder.

ISBN: 1-84273-811-9

Printed in China

Produced by the Bridgewater Book Company Ltd

**Photographer** Calvey Taylor-Haw

**Home Economist** Ricky Taylor

The crockery featured on the following pages can be
purchased at Marks and Spencer's stores:

page 11 – light green with yellow rim bowl & plate,
        02148/4925/108 & 02148/4923/108

page 17 – white bowl, 02733/4285

page 53 – blue and white bowl & plate,
        02733/1002 & 02733/1005

pages 67 & 93 – silver-rimmed plate, 02148/5306

## NOTES FOR THE READER

- This book uses both metric and imperial measurements. Follow the same units of measurement throughout; do not mix metric and imperial.

- All spoon measurements are level: teaspoons are assumed to be 5 ml, and tablespoons are assumed to be 15 ml.

- Unless otherwise stated, milk is assumed to be full fat, eggs and individual vegetables such as potatoes are medium, and pepper is freshly ground black pepper.

- Recipes using raw or very lightly cooked eggs should be avoided by infants, the elderly, pregnant women, convalescents, and anyone suffering from an illness.

- The times given are an approximate guide only. Preparation times differ according to the techniques used by different people and the cooking times may also vary from those given. Optional ingredients, variations or serving suggestions have not been included in the calculations.

# contents

# introduction

Fish and shellfish are superbly healthy foods. Always buy and use only the freshest fish and shellfish, and you will find that their value in terms of health, quality and flavour is hard to beat. They are low in calories, yet rich in nutrients such as B vitamins and proteins. Oily fish in particular, such as salmon and anchovies, are a good source of omega-3 oils, which the body cannot produce for itself. These oils have anti-inflammatory properties and are believed to be very beneficial for maintaining a healthy heart.

Fish and shellfish are excellent sources of other nutrients too, such as iodine, which is essential for a healthy thyroid gland and efficient metabolism; co-enzyme Q10, which strengthens muscle and protects against heart disease and diabetes; zinc, which is essential in the synthesis of DNA and helps repair tissue; and magnesium, which plays an important role in the formation of bone, and in energy production and insulin regulation.

Many types of fish and shellfish, such as cod and tuna, prawns and mussels, are low in fat, and can be invaluable as part of a weight control regime. But most of all, we shouldn't forget that fish is delicious and wonderfully versatile. So whatever the occasion, there will be something here to satisfy every palate.

| guide to recipe key | |
|---|---|
| very easy | Recipes are graded as follows: 1 pea = easy; 2 peas = very easy; 3 peas = extremely easy. |
| serves 4 | Recipes generally serve four people. Simply halve the ingredients to serve two, taking care not to mix metric and imperial measurements. |
| 10 minutes | Preparation time. Where marinating, chilling or cooling are involved, these times have been added on separately: eg, 15 minutes + 30 minutes to marinate. |
| 10 minutes | Cooking time. Cooking times don't include the cooking of side dishes or accompaniments served with the main dishes. |

cod & sweet potato soup
page 10

prawn cocktail
page 36

crab & citrus salsa
page 56

salmon with brandy sauce
page 72

# soups
# & stews

Fish soups make a delicious start to any meal, or a light meal in themselves when served with some fresh crusty bread and a side salad. And when appetites are large, what could be more satisfying than a simmering fish stew full of tantalising flavours and mouthwatering ingredients? This chapter presents a collection of recipes with international flavours from countries such as France, Spain and Thailand, and all are quick and easy to make.

# haddock soup à la provençal

|  | ingredients | |
|---|---|---|
| very easy | 1 tbsp extra-virgin olive oil | 200 ml/7 fl oz red wine |
|  | 2 red onions, chopped | 1 litre/1¾ pints vegetable stock |
| serves 4 | 2 garlic cloves, finely chopped | 1 bay leaf |
|  | 1 carrot, chopped | 350 g/12 oz haddock fillets, skinned |
|  | 1 red pepper, deseeded and chopped | salt and pepper |
| 15 minutes | 6 tomatoes | |
|  | 1 tbsp tomato purée | fresh basil, chopped, to garnish |
|  | 1 tsp turmeric | fresh baguettes, to serve |
| 1 hour 10 minutes | | |

Heat the oil in a large pan over a medium heat. Add the onions and cook, stirring from time to time, for about 4 minutes. Add the garlic, carrot, red pepper, tomatoes, tomato purée and turmeric and cook, stirring occasionally, for another 4 minutes. Stir in the wine, then the stock. Add the bay leaf and bring to the boil. Lower the heat and simmer for 25 minutes, stirring occasionally.

Rinse the haddock fillets under cold running water, then add them to the soup. Season with salt and pepper and cook for another 25 minutes until the fish is cooked through.

Remove the pan from the heat, let the soup cool a little, then discard the bay leaf. Transfer the soup to a food processor and process until smooth (you may need to do this in batches). Return the soup to the pan and bring gently to the boil again. Lower the heat and simmer for 5 minutes. Ladle the soup into serving bowls, garnish with basil and serve with fresh baguettes.

# cod & sweet potato soup

| | |
|---|---|
| very easy | |
| serves 4 | |
| 15 minutes + 30 minutes to marinate | |
| 40 minutes | |

### ingredients

4 tbsp lemon juice
1 red chilli, deseeded and finely sliced
pinch of nutmeg
250 g/9 oz cod fillets, skinned
1 tbsp vegetable oil
1 onion, chopped
4 spring onions, trimmed and chopped
2 garlic cloves, chopped

450 g/1 lb sweet potatoes, diced
1 litre/1¾ pints vegetable stock
salt and pepper
1 carrot, sliced
150 g/5½ oz white cabbage, shredded
2 celery sticks, trimmed and sliced

fresh crusty bread, to serve

Put the lemon juice, chilli and nutmeg into a shallow, non-metallic (glass or ceramic) dish and mix to make a marinade. Rinse the cod, cut it into chunks and add to the bowl. Turn in the marinade until coated. Cover with clingfilm and leave to marinate for 30 minutes.

Heat the oil in a large pan over a medium heat. Add the onion and spring onions and cook, stirring, for 4 minutes. Add the garlic and cook for 2 minutes.

Add the sweet potato, pour in the stock and season. Bring to the boil, lower the heat, cover and simmer for 10 minutes. Add the carrot, cabbage and celery, season again, and simmer for 8–10 minutes. Remove from the heat and allow to cool a little.

Process the soup in a food processor until smooth (you may need to do this in batches), then return to the pan. Add the fish chunks and marinade and bring gently to the boil. Lower the heat and simmer for 10 minutes. Ladle the soup into bowls and serve with crusty bread.

# bouillabaisse

| | ingredients | |
|---|---|---|
| easy | 250 g/9 oz cod or haddock fillets | 1 bay leaf |
| | 250 g/9 oz sea bass fillets | pinch of saffron threads |
| | 6 tbsp olive oil | 150 g/5$\frac{1}{2}$ oz potatoes |
| serves 4 | 4 garlic cloves, chopped | 100 g/3$\frac{1}{2}$ oz live mussels, soaked and |
| | 2 onions, sliced | cleaned (see page 20) |
| | 1 small red chilli, deseeded and chopped | 100 g/3$\frac{1}{2}$ oz scallops |
| 20 minutes | 2 celery sticks, trimmed and sliced | 300 g/10$\frac{1}{2}$ oz prawns, peeled and |
| | 1 green pepper, deseeded and sliced | deveined |
| | 4 tomatoes, sliced | fresh parsley, chopped, to garnish |
| 1 hour 10 minutes | 1 litre/1$\frac{3}{4}$ pints fish stock | |
| | 100 ml/3$\frac{1}{2}$ fl oz dry white wine | slices of French bread, to serve |

Rinse the fish fillets, cut into chunks and put them in a shallow dish. Mix 3 tablespoons of oil with 1 chopped garlic clove and pour over the fish. Cover with clingfilm and refrigerate. Heat 1 tablespoon of oil in a pan. Add 1 onion and the chilli, celery and green pepper. Cook over a medium heat for 4 minutes. Add the tomatoes, stock, wine, bay leaf and saffron. Bring to the boil, cover and simmer for 30 minutes. Strain and reserve the liquid. Heat the remaining oil in a pan. Add the remaining garlic and onion and cook for 4 minutes. Slice and add the potatoes and strained stock. Bring to the boil, lower the heat to medium, cover and cook for 15 minutes.

Put the mussels in a pan with a little water, bring to the boil and cook over a high heat for 4 minutes. Discard any that remain closed. Add the fish chunks to the potato pan. Cook for 2 minutes. Add the mussels, scallops and prawns. Cook for 4 minutes. Transfer to serving bowls, garnish with parsley and serve with slices of French bread.

# thai prawn & scallop soup

| | | ingredients | | |
|---|---|---|---|---|
| | very easy | 1 litre/1¾ pints fish stock | | 225 g/8 oz prawns, peeled and |
| | | juice of ½ lime | | deveined |
| | serves 4 | 2 tbsp rice wine or sherry | | 225 g/8 oz scallops |
| | | 1 leek, trimmed and sliced | | 1½ tbsp chopped fresh flat-leaved |
| | | 2 shallots, finely chopped | | parsley |
| | | 1 tbsp grated fresh root ginger | | salt and pepper |
| | 5 minutes | 1 red chilli, deseeded and finely | | |
| | | chopped | | fresh flat-leaved parsley, chopped, |
| | | | | to garnish |
| | 15 minutes | | | |

Put the stock, lime juice, rice wine or sherry, leek, shallots, ginger and chilli into a large saucepan. Bring to the boil, then lower the heat, cover and simmer for 10 minutes.

Add the prawns, scallops and parsley, season with salt and pepper, and cook for about 1–2 minutes.

Remove the pan from the heat, ladle the soup into serving bowls, garnish with chopped fresh parsley and serve.

# chorizo & scallop soup

| | |
|---|---|
| very easy | |
| serves 4 | |
| 10 minutes | |
| 1¼–1½ hours | |

### ingredients

125 g/4½ oz lean chorizo, skinned and chopped
450 g/1 lb split yellow peas
1 tbsp vegetable oil
2 shallots, chopped
2 carrots, chopped
2 leeks, trimmed and chopped
2 garlic cloves, chopped

1.5 litres/2¾ pints vegetable stock
½ tsp dried oregano
salt and pepper
225 g/8 oz scallops

fresh flat-leaved parsley, chopped, to garnish

slices of fresh wholemeal bread, to serve

Put the chorizo in a clean, dry frying pan and cook over a medium heat for about 5–8 minutes. Lift out with a slotted spoon and drain on kitchen paper. Put the peas in a colander and rinse under cold running water. Leave to drain.

Heat the oil in a large saucepan over a medium heat. Add the shallots and cook for about 4 minutes, until slightly softened. Add the carrots, leeks and garlic and cook for another 3 minutes.

Add the drained peas to the pan, then the stock and oregano. Bring to the boil, then add the chorizo and season with salt and pepper. Lower the heat, cover and simmer for 1–1¼ hours. Just before the end of the cooking time, add the scallops and cook for about 2 minutes.

Remove the saucepan from the heat. Ladle the soup into serving bowls, garnish with chopped fresh parsley and serve with slices of fresh wholemeal bread.

# spicy crab & vegetable soup

| | | ingredients | |
|---|---|---|---|
| | very easy | 500 g/1 lb 2 oz tomatoes | 200 g/7 oz canned or freshly cooked |
| | | 1 litre/1¾ pints fish or vegetable stock | crab meat |
| | | 4 tsp red wine | 150 g/5½ oz canned sweetcorn |
| | serves 4 | 150 g/5½ oz red cabbage, shredded | 4 tbsp chopped fresh flat-leaved |
| | | 2 red onions, sliced | parsley |
| | | 2 carrots, cut into matchsticks | salt and pepper |
| | 15 minutes | 3 garlic cloves, chopped | |
| | | 1 small red chilli, deseeded and finely | fresh flat-leaved parsley, chopped, |
| | | chopped | to garnish |
| | 35 minutes | 1 bay leaf | fresh crusty baguettes, to serve |

Put the tomatoes into a heatproof bowl, cover with boiling water and leave for 1 minute. Drain, plunge into cold water, then remove the skins – they should come off easily.

Chop the tomatoes, then put them into a large saucepan. Pour over the stock, then add the wine, cabbage, onions, carrots, garlic, chilli and bay leaf. Bring to the boil, then lower the heat and simmer for about 15 minutes.

Add the crab meat, sweetcorn and parsley to the pan, and season with salt and plenty of pepper. Cook gently over a low heat for a further 15 minutes.

Remove the saucepan from the heat and discard the bay leaf. Ladle the soup into serving bowls, garnish with chopped fresh parsley and serve with fresh crusty baguettes.

# fruits de mer stew

| | |
|---|---|
| easy | |
| serves 4 | |
| 15 minutes | |
| 30 minutes | |

## ingredients

3 tbsp olive oil
2 garlic cloves, chopped
3 spring onions, trimmed and chopped
1 red pepper, deseeded and chopped
425 g/15 oz canned chopped tomatoes
1 tbsp tomato purée
1 bay leaf
$\frac{1}{2}$ tsp dried mixed herbs
200 g/7 oz live mussels
150 g/5$\frac{1}{2}$ oz cod fillet, skinned
150 g/5$\frac{1}{2}$ oz swordfish steak, skinned

350 ml/12 fl oz fish stock
4 tbsp red wine
salt and pepper
200 g/7 oz canned crab meat
200 g/7 oz prawns, peeled and deveined
250 g/9 oz cooked lobster meat

GARNISH
fresh flat-leaved parsley, chopped
slices of lemon

slices of French bread, to serve

Heat the oil in a pan over a low heat. Add the garlic, spring onions and red pepper and cook, stirring, for 4 minutes. Add the tomatoes, tomato purée, bay leaf and mixed herbs. Cook for 10 minutes.

Meanwhile, soak the mussels in lightly salted water for 10 minutes. Scrub under cold running water and pull off any beards. Discard any with broken shells. Tap the remaining mussels and discard any that refuse to close. Put them in a large pan with a little water, bring to the boil and cook over a high heat for 4 minutes. Remove from the heat, drain and discard any mussels that remain closed.

Cut the cod and swordfish into chunks and add to the tomato pan. Add the stock and wine. Season and bring to the boil. Add the mussels and crab, lower the heat, cover and cook for 5 minutes. Add the prawns and cook for 3 minutes. Cut the lobster into chunks, add to the pan and cook for 2 minutes. Transfer to bowls, garnish with parsley and lemon slices and serve with slices of French bread.

# spanish swordfish stew

| | |
|---|---|
| very easy | |
| serves 4 | |
| 10 minutes | |
| 55 minutes | |

## ingredients

4 tbsp olive oil
3 shallots, chopped
2 garlic cloves, chopped
225 g/8 oz canned chopped tomatoes
1 tbsp tomato purée
650 g/1 lb 7 oz potatoes, sliced
250 ml/9 fl oz vegetable stock
2 tbsp lemon juice
1 red pepper, deseeded and chopped
1 orange pepper, deseeded and
    chopped

20 black olives, stoned and halved
1 kg/2 lb 4 oz swordfish steak, skinned
    and cut into bite-sized pieces
salt and pepper

GARNISH
sprigs of fresh flat-leaved parsley
slices of lemon

fresh crusty bread, to serve

Heat the oil in a saucepan over a low heat. Add the shallots and cook, stirring occasionally, for about 4 minutes, until slightly softened. Add the garlic, tomatoes and tomato purée, cover and cook gently for 20 minutes.

Put the potatoes into a flameproof casserole with the stock and lemon juice. Bring to the boil, then lower the heat and add the peppers. Cover and cook for 15 minutes.

Add the olives, swordfish and the tomato mixture to the potatoes. Season with salt and pepper. Stir the stew, cover and simmer for 7–10 minutes, or until the swordfish is cooked to your taste.

Remove from the heat and garnish with sprigs of fresh parsley and lemon slices. Serve with fresh crusty bread.

# salads

Whoever said that salads are dull? This chapter offers some exciting recipes for you to try. For example, the Anchovy & Olive Salad shows just how well olives and fish go together, and the Warm Tuna & Kidney Bean Salad demonstrates how salads can be every bit as warming as a hot meal. Some salads in this chapter are light dishes that would make excellent starters or accompaniments to main courses. Others have extra ingredients added, such as tenderly cooked pasta, to make them into more substantial meals.

# tuna & herbed fusilli salad

| | | ingredients | |
|---|---|---|---|
| extremely easy | | 200 g/7 oz dried fusilli<br>1 red pepper, deseeded and cut<br>　into quarters<br>150 g/5½ oz fresh asparagus spears<br>1 red onion, sliced<br>4 tomatoes, sliced<br>200 g/7 oz canned tuna in brine,<br>　drained | DRESSING<br>6 tbsp basil-flavoured oil or extra-<br>　virgin olive oil<br>3 tbsp white wine vinegar<br>1 tbsp lime juice<br>1 tsp mustard<br>1 tsp honey<br>4 tbsp chopped fresh basil |
| serves 4 | | | |
| 15 minutes | | | sprigs of fresh basil, to garnish |
| 15 minutes | | | |

Bring a large pan of lightly salted water to the boil. Cook the fusilli for 10 minutes, or according to the instructions on the packet. The pasta should be tender but still firm to the bite. While it is cooking, put the pepper quarters under a grill and cook until the skins have begun to blacken. Transfer to a polythene bag, seal and set aside.

Bring another pan of water to the boil and cook the asparagus for 4 minutes. Drain and plunge into cold water, then drain again. Remove the pasta from the heat, drain and set aside to cool. Take the red pepper quarters from the bag and remove the blackened skins. Slice the peppers into strips.

To make the dressing, put all the ingredients into a large bowl and stir together well. Add the pasta, pepper strips, asparagus, onion, tomatoes and tuna. Toss together gently then divide between serving bowls. Garnish with sprigs of fresh basil and serve.

# smoked salmon,
# asparagus & avocado salad

| | | **ingredients** | |
|---|---|---|---|
| | very easy | 200 g/7 oz fresh asparagus spears | 4 tbsp extra-virgin olive oil |
| | | 1 large ripe avocado | 2 tbsp white wine vinegar |
| | | 1 tbsp lemon juice | 1 tbsp lemon juice |
| | serves 4 | large handful fresh rocket leaves | pinch of sugar |
| | | 225 g/8 oz smoked salmon slices | 1 tsp mustard |
| | | 1 red onion, finely sliced | |
| | 15 minutes | 1 tbsp chopped fresh parsley | GARNISH |
| | | 1 tbsp chopped fresh chives | sprigs of fresh flat-leaved parsley |
| | | | wedges of lemon |
| | 5 minutes | DRESSING | |
| | | 1 garlic clove, chopped | fresh wholemeal bread, to serve |

Bring a large saucepan of salted water to the boil. Add the asparagus and cook for 4 minutes, then drain. Refresh under cold running water and drain again. Set aside to cool.

To make the dressing, combine all the ingredients in a small bowl and stir together well. Cut the avocado in half lengthways, then remove and discard the stone and skin. Cut the flesh into bite-sized pieces and brush with lemon juice to prevent discoloration.

To assemble the salad, arrange the rocket leaves on individual serving plates and top with the asparagus and avocado. Cut the smoked salmon into strips and scatter over the top of the salad, then scatter over the onion and herbs. Drizzle over the dressing, then garnish with fresh parsley sprigs and lemon wedges. Serve with fresh wholemeal bread.

# warm tuna & kidney bean salad

| | | **ingredients** | |
|---|---|---|---|
| extremely easy | | 4 fresh tuna steaks, about 175 g/6 oz each | DRESSING |
| | | 1 tbsp olive oil | 5 tbsp extra-virgin olive oil |
| serves 4 | | salt and pepper | 3 tbsp balsamic vinegar |
| | | 200 g/7 oz canned kidney beans | 1 tbsp lime juice |
| | | 100 g/3½ oz canned sweetcorn | 1 garlic clove, chopped |
| 10 minutes | | 2 spring onions, trimmed and thinly sliced | 1 tbsp chopped fresh coriander |
| | | | salt and pepper |
| | | | GARNISH |
| 5–10 minutes | | | sprigs of fresh coriander |
| | | | wedges of lime |

Preheat a ridged griddle pan. While the pan is heating, brush the tuna steaks with olive oil, then season with salt and pepper. Cook the steaks for 2 minutes, then turn them over and cook on the other side for a further 2 minutes, or according to your taste, but do not overcook. Remove from the heat and allow to cool slightly.

While the tuna is cooling, heat the kidney beans and sweetcorn according to the instructions on the cans, then drain.

To make the dressing, put all the ingredients into a small bowl and stir together well.

Put the kidney beans, sweetcorn and spring onions into a large bowl, pour over half of the dressing and mix together well. Divide the bean and sweetcorn salad between individual serving plates, then place a tuna steak on each one. Drizzle over the remaining dressing, garnish with the fresh coriander sprigs and lime wedges, and serve.

# anchovy & olive salad

| | | **ingredients** | |
|---|---|---|---|
| extremely easy | | large handful mixed lettuce leaves<br>12 cherry tomatoes, halved<br>20 black olives, stoned and halved<br>6 canned anchovy fillets, drained<br>  and thinly sliced<br>1 tbsp chopped fresh oregano | DRESSING<br>4 tbsp extra-virgin olive oil<br>1 tbsp white wine vinegar<br>1 tbsp lemon juice<br>1 tbsp chopped fresh flat-leaved<br>  parsley<br>salt and pepper |
| serves 4 | | | |
| 10 minutes | | | wedges of lemon, to garnish |
| — | | | |

To make the dressing, put all the ingredients into a small bowl, season with salt and pepper and stir together well.

To assemble the salad, arrange the lettuce leaves in a serving dish. Scatter the cherry tomatoes on top, followed by the olives, anchovies and oregano. Drizzle over the dressing. Serve on individual plates garnished with lemon wedges.

# seafood & spinach salad

| | | ingredients |
|---|---|---|
| very easy | 500 g/1 lb 2 oz live mussels, soaked and cleaned (see page 20) | 1 tbsp lemon juice |
| | 100 g/3½ oz prawns, peeled and | 1 tsp finely grated lemon rind |
| serves 4 | deveined | 1 garlic clove, chopped |
| | 350 g/12 oz scallops | 1 tbsp grated fresh root ginger |
| | 500 g/1 lb 2 oz baby spinach leaves | 1 small red chilli, deseeded and sliced |
| 25 minutes + 45 minutes to chill | 3 spring onions, trimmed and sliced | 1 tbsp chopped fresh coriander |
| | | salt and pepper |
| | DRESSING | GARNISH |
| 10 minutes | 4 tbsp extra-virgin olive oil | sprigs of fresh coriander |
| | 2 tbsp white wine vinegar | wedges of lemon |

Put the mussels into a large pan with a little water, bring to the boil and cook over a high heat for 4 minutes. Drain and reserve the liquid. Discard any mussels that remain closed. Return the reserved liquid to the pan and bring to the boil. Add the prawns and scallops and cook for 3 minutes. Drain. Remove the mussels from their shells. Rinse the mussels, prawns and scallops in cold water, drain and put them in a large bowl. Cool, cover with clingfilm and chill for 45 minutes. Meanwhile, rinse the baby spinach leaves and transfer them to a pan with 4 tablespoons of water. Cook over a high heat for 1 minute, transfer to a colander, refresh under cold running water and drain.

To make the dressing, put all the ingredients into a small bowl and mix. Arrange the spinach on serving dishes, then scatter over half of the spring onions. Top with the mussels, prawns and scallops, then scatter over the remaining spring onions. Drizzle over the dressing, garnish with fresh coriander sprigs and wedges of lemon and serve.

# prawn cocktail

| | | ingredients | |
|---|---|---|---|
| very easy | | 1 avocado | 300 ml/10 fl oz sunflower oil |
| | | 1 tbsp lemon juice | 100 ml/3 $\frac{1}{2}$ fl oz tomato ketchup |
| serves 4 | | 500 g/1 lb 2 oz cooked prawns, peeled | |
| | | | GARNISH |
| | | DRESSING | pinch of paprika |
| | | 1 egg | strips of lemon zest |
| 10 minutes | | 2 tsp sherry vinegar | 4 whole cooked prawns, optional |
| | | $\frac{1}{2}$ tsp mustard | |
| | | dash of Worcestershire sauce | fresh green lettuce leaves, to serve |
| — | | pinch of salt | |

To make the dressing, break the egg into a food processor. Add the vinegar, mustard, Worcestershire sauce and salt and process for 15 seconds. While the motor is running, slowly pour the sunflower oil through the feeder tube until thoroughly incorporated. Transfer the dressing to a large bowl, then stir in the tomato ketchup. Cover with clingfilm and chill in the refrigerator until required.

Cut the avocado in half lengthways, then remove and discard the stone and skin. Cut the flesh into slices, then brush the slices with lemon juice to prevent discoloration.

To assemble the salad, take the dressing from the refrigerator, add the avocado and prawns and stir gently until coated.

Divide the lettuce leaves between large individual serving glasses or bowls. Fill each one with prawns, then garnish with paprika and lemon zest strips. If using whole prawns, hang a whole cooked prawn on the rim of each glass or bowl. Serve immediately.

# light meals

Fish and shellfish make wonderful light meals. This chapter presents recipes with a wide range of international flavours from places as far apart as South America, Europe and Asia. The dishes are all easy to prepare and quick to cook, and are full of nutritious ingredients. Some are deliciously light yet satisfying, such as Monkfish & Asparagus Stir-fry, while others are irresistibly rich, such as Mediterranean Mussels in Cream. Many of these dishes would make superb lunches or light suppers.

# monkfish & asparagus stir-fry

| | | **ingredients** | |
|---|---|---|---|
| | very easy | 500 g/1 lb 2 oz monkfish | 100 g/3½ oz mangetouts |
| | | 4 tbsp vegetable oil | 6 tbsp plain flour |
| | serves 4 | 2 courgettes, trimmed, halved and sliced | 4 tbsp lemon sauce (available ready-made from supermarkets and oriental food shops) |
| | | 1 red pepper, deseeded and sliced | 1 tbsp freshly grated lemon grass |
| | 15 minutes | 2 garlic cloves, finely chopped | 1 tbsp grated fresh root ginger |
| | | 150 g/5½ oz fresh asparagus spears | salt and pepper |
| | 15 minutes | | |

Remove any membrane from the monkfish, then cut the flesh into thin slices. Cover with clingfilm and set aside. Heat 2 tablespoons of the oil in a wok or large frying pan until hot. Add the courgettes and stir-fry for 2 minutes. Add the red pepper and garlic and cook for another 2 minutes. Add the asparagus and cook for 1 minute, then add the mangetouts and cook for 2 minutes. Transfer the vegetables onto a plate.

Put the flour in a shallow dish and turn the fish slices in the flour until coated. Heat the remaining oil in the wok or frying pan. Add the fish and stir-fry for 5 minutes, or until cooked to your taste (you may need to do this in batches). Transfer the fish to another plate.

Put the lemon sauce, lemon grass and ginger in the wok or frying pan. Add the fish and stir-fry over a medium heat for a few seconds. Add the vegetables and stir-fry for 1 minute. Season, stir again and remove from the heat. Transfer to warm plates and serve.

# thai fish burgers

| | | ingredients | |
|---|---|---|---|
| very easy | | 350 g/12 oz haddock fillets, skinned and cut into small pieces | 2 tbsp chopped fresh coriander<br>1 tbsp groundnut oil |
| serves 4 | | 25 g/1 oz almonds, chopped<br>25 g/1 oz fresh breadcrumbs<br>½ onion, finely chopped | TO SERVE<br>hamburger buns |
| 15 minutes | | 1 red chilli, deseeded and finely chopped<br>1 egg white | slices of tomato<br>selection of fresh green salad leaves |
| 5–6 minutes | | 1 tbsp soy sauce<br>1 tbsp finely chopped lemon grass | |

Put the haddock, almonds, breadcrumbs, onion, chilli, egg white, soy sauce, lemon grass and coriander into a large bowl and stir together. Put the mixture into a food processor and process until thoroughly blended. Transfer to a clean work surface and, using your hands, shape the mixture into flat, round burger shapes.

Heat the oil in a frying pan and add the burgers. Cook for about 5 minutes, turning once, until cooked through.

Remove from the heat. Serve with hamburger buns stuffed with tomato slices and crisp lettuce, and a green side salad.

# haddock nachos

| | |
|---|---|
| very easy | |
| serves 4 | |
| 10 minutes | |
| 15 minutes | |

### ingredients

butter, for greasing
650 g/1 lb 7 oz haddock fillets, skinned
4 tomatoes, chopped
1 onion, chopped
1 tbsp lime juice
salt and pepper
50 g/1¾ oz tortilla chips

100 g/3½ oz smoked firm cheese (such
 as Applewood), grated

sprigs of fresh coriander, to garnish

TO SERVE
125 ml/4 fl oz soured cream
fresh crusty bread

Preheat the oven to 200°C/400°F/Gas Mark 6. Grease a large baking dish with butter.

Rinse the haddock fillets under cold running water, then pat them dry with kitchen paper. Arrange the fillets in the bottom of the baking dish.

In a separate bowl, mix together the tomatoes, onion and lime juice. Season with salt and pepper, then spread the mixture over the fish fillets. Scatter the tortilla chips over the top, then sprinkle over the grated cheese.

Bake in the centre of the preheated oven for about 15 minutes. Remove from the oven and transfer to serving plates. Garnish with sprigs of coriander. Serve with the soured cream and fresh bread.

# mediterranean mussels in cream

| | ingredients | |
|---|---|---|
| very easy | 2 tbsp butter | sprigs of fresh flat-leaved parsley, |
| | 1 onion, chopped | to garnish |
| | 2 spring onions, chopped | |
| serves 4 | 2 garlic cloves, chopped | |
| | 1 kg/2 lb 4 oz live mussels, soaked and | |
| | cleaned (see page 20) | |
| 15 minutes | 100 ml/3½ fl oz dry white wine | |
| | 3 tbsp chopped fresh parsley | |
| | 150 ml/5 fl oz single cream | |
| 20 minutes | | |

Melt the butter in a large saucepan over a low heat. Add the onion, spring onions and garlic, and cook for 3 minutes until the onion has softened slightly. Increase the heat to medium, add the mussels, cover and cook for 4–5 minutes.

Remove the pan from the heat. Using a slotted spoon, lift out the mussels and discard any that have not opened. Set the remaining mussels to one side. Return the pan to the heat, stir in the wine and parsley and bring to the boil. Continue to cook, stirring, for about 10 minutes.

Arrange the mussels in serving bowls, then remove the sauce from the heat. Stir in the cream, pour the sauce over the mussels, garnish with parsley sprigs and serve.

# oriental deep-fried prawns

| | **ingredients** | |
|---|---|---|
| very easy | 4 tbsp chilli oil | 1 small red chilli, deseeded and chopped |
| | 4 spring onions, trimmed and finely chopped | 1 tbsp grated fresh root ginger |
| serves 4 | 450 g/1 lb fresh prawns, peeled and deveined | 2 tbsp rice wine or sherry |
| | 200 g/7 oz canned water chestnuts, drained and sliced | 2 tbsp chopped fresh coriander |
| | | salt and pepper |
| 10 minutes | 1 tbsp freshly grated lemon grass | GARNISH |
| | 1 red pepper, deseeded and finely chopped | fresh coriander, finely chopped |
| 10–12 minutes | | slices of lime |
| | | freshly cooked jasmine rice, to serve |

Heat the oil in a frying pan and add the spring onions. Cook over a medium heat for 3 minutes until slightly softened.

Add the prawns, water chestnuts, lemon grass, red pepper, chilli, ginger, rice wine and coriander. Season with salt and pepper. Cook, stirring, for 5–7 minutes, or according to your taste. Garnish with finely chopped coriander and slices of lime, and serve with freshly cooked jasmine rice.

# spicy crab tortillas

| | | **ingredients** | |
|---|---|---|---|
| | very easy | 1 tbsp chilli oil | 1 tbsp chopped fresh coriander |
| | | 1 large onion, roughly chopped | salt and pepper |
| | serves 4 | 2 garlic cloves, chopped | 8 small wheat or corn tortillas |
| | | 250 g/9 oz canned or freshly cooked crab meat | sprigs of fresh coriander, to garnish |
| | 10 minutes | 1 small red chilli, deseeded and finely chopped | 125 ml/4 fl oz soured cream, to serve |
| | | 2 tomatoes, chopped | |
| | 15 minutes | | |

Heat the oil in a frying pan and add the onion and garlic. Cook over a medium heat for about 3–4 minutes until the onion is slightly softened.

Add the crab meat, chilli, tomatoes and coriander. Season with salt and pepper. Cook, stirring, for 10 minutes, or according to your taste. About a minute before the crab is ready, warm the tortillas in a dry frying pan for a few seconds.

Remove the crab mixture and the tortillas from the heat. Spread a spoonful of soured cream onto each tortilla, add some of the crab mixture and roll up. Garnish with coriander sprigs and serve at once.

# devilled prawns

| | | ingredients | |
|---|---|---|---|
| very easy | | 4 tbsp groundnut oil | pinch of paprika |
| | | 4 spring onions, trimmed and finely sliced | 1 tsp red food colouring, optional |
| serves 4 | | 450 g/1 lb fresh prawns, peeled and deveined | salt and pepper |
| | | 1 small red chilli, deseeded and finely sliced | fresh coriander stalks, finely sliced, to garnish |
| 10 minutes | | 2 tbsp sherry | freshly boiled rice, to serve |
| 10–12 minutes | | | |

Heat the oil in a frying pan and add the spring onions. Cook over a medium heat for 3 minutes until slightly softened.

Add the prawns, chilli, sherry, paprika, red food colouring (if using), and salt and pepper to taste. Cook, stirring, for about 5–7 minutes, or according to your taste. Garnish with finely sliced coriander stalks and serve with freshly boiled rice.

# grilled sardines
# with lemon & coriander

| | | ingredients | |
|---|---|---|---|
| very easy | 12 sardines, scaled and gutted | 2 tbsp white wine vinegar |
| | 1 tbsp olive oil | 4 tbsp chopped fresh coriander |
| serves 4 | DRESSING | pepper |
| | 1 garlic clove, finely chopped | GARNISH |
| | 3 spring onions, trimmed and sliced | slices of fresh lemon |
| 10 minutes | 125 ml/4 fl oz extra-virgin olive oil | sprigs of fresh coriander |
| | 4 tbsp lemon juice | |
| 6 minutes | | |

Preheat the grill to medium. Rinse the fish inside and out under cold running water. Drain, then pat dry with kitchen paper.

To make the dressing, put the garlic, spring onions, olive oil, lemon juice, vinegar and coriander into a small bowl and mix together well. Season with plenty of pepper and set aside.

Line a grill pan with aluminium foil, then brush the foil with a little olive oil. Arrange the sardines on the foil, then spoon some of the dressing inside each fish. Brush more dressing on the top of the sardines and cook under the preheated grill for about 3 minutes. Turn the fish over, brush with more dressing and cook for a further 3 minutes, or until cooked through.

Remove from the grill, transfer onto individual serving plates and garnish with lemon slices and coriander sprigs.

# crab & citrus salsa

| | | **ingredients** | |
|---|---|---|---|
| very easy | 250 g/9 oz canned or freshly cooked | GARNISH | |
| | | crab meat | sprigs of fresh flat-leaved parsley |
| | 1 red pepper, deseeded and chopped | wedges of lime | |
| serves 4 | 4 tomatoes, chopped | | |
| | 3 spring onions, trimmed and chopped | TO SERVE | |
| | 1 tbsp chopped fresh flat-leaved parsley | carrots, cut into matchsticks | |
| 10 minutes | 1 red chilli, deseeded and chopped | celery sticks, cut into matchsticks | |
| + 30 minutes | 3 tbsp lime juice | tortilla chips | |
| to chill | 3 tbsp orange juice | | |
| — | salt and pepper | | |

Put the crab meat, red pepper, tomatoes, spring onions, parsley and chilli into a large non-metallic (glass or ceramic) bowl, which will not react with acid. Add the lime juice and orange juice, season with salt and pepper and mix well. Cover with clingfilm and refrigerate for 30 minutes to allow the flavours to combine.

Remove the salsa from the refrigerator. Garnish with parsley sprigs and wedges of lime and serve with carrots, celery and tortilla chips for dipping.

# scallop bake

| | |
|---|---|
| very easy | |
| serves 4 | |
| 10 minutes | |
| 25 minutes | |

### ingredients

100 g/3½ oz dried tagliatelle
2 tbsp butter, plus extra for greasing
500 g/1 lb 2 oz scallops
2 tbsp plain flour
2 tbsp milk
250 ml/9 fl oz single cream
salt and pepper
100 g/3½ oz cooked ham, diced

2 spring onions, trimmed and finely
  chopped
25 g/1 oz Parmesan cheese, freshly
  grated

TO SERVE
selection of fresh salad leaves
slices of fresh bread

Cook the tagliatelle according to the instructions on the packet. While the pasta is cooking, preheat the oven to 180°C/350°F/Gas Mark 4. Grease a large baking dish with butter. Bring a pan of water to the boil, add the scallops and cook them for 2 minutes. Drain the scallops and set aside.

Put the remaining butter into a saucepan and melt it gently over a low heat. Add the flour and cook, stirring, for 2 minutes. Pour in the milk, then stir in the cream. Season with salt and pepper and simmer for another 2 minutes.

Drain the tagliatelle well, then arrange it on the bottom of the baking dish. Layer the scallops over the top, followed by the ham and spring onions. Pour over the cream sauce, then sprinkle over the Parmesan cheese. Bake in the centre of the preheated oven for about 15 minutes, until golden on top. Serve with a side salad of mixed leaves and slices of fresh bread.

# sautéed prawns with whisky

| | |
|---|---|
| very easy | |
| serves 4 | |
| 10 minutes | |
| 8–10 minutes | |

## ingredients

75 g/2¾ oz plain flour
pinch of salt
pinch of paprika
700 g/1 lb 9 oz fresh prawns, peeled and deveined
4 tbsp vegetable oil
3 garlic cloves, finely chopped

1 spring onion, trimmed and finely chopped
2 tbsp chopped fresh coriander
1 tbsp chopped fresh marjoram
4 tbsp whisky
pepper

TO SERVE
crisp green and red salad leaves
fresh baguettes

Put the flour, salt and paprika into a large bowl and mix together well. Add the prawns and turn them in the mixture until coated.

Heat the oil in a frying pan and add the prawns, garlic, spring onion, herbs and whisky. Season with pepper, and stir together. Cook over a medium heat, turning frequently, for 5 minutes. Remove the pan from the heat and arrange the prawn mixture on a heatproof serving dish.

To finish, place the dish under a grill preheated to medium and cook for 2–3 minutes. Serve with crisp green and red salad leaves and fresh baguettes.

# main meals

The dishes in this chapter are truly a feast for the eyes and the palate. Inspiration for these recipes has come from places as diverse as the Scottish Highlands and the Far East. From kedgeree to curry, and from gratin to barbecue, the sheer variety of ingredients and cooking methods in this section will entice experienced cooks and novices alike, and provide a culinary treat that everyone will remember.

# grilled halibut with garlic butter

| | | **ingredients** | |
|---|---|---|---|
| extremely easy | 4 halibut fillets, about 175 g/6 oz each | GARNISH | |
| | 6 tbsp butter, plus extra for greasing | sprigs of fresh parsley | |
| | salt and pepper | thin strips of orange zest | |
| serves 4 | 2 garlic cloves, finely chopped | | |
| | | TO SERVE | |
| 5 minutes | | crisp salad leaves | |
| | | cherry tomatoes, cut into slices | |
| 7–8 minutes | | | |

Preheat the grill to medium. Rinse the fish fillets under cold running water, then pat dry with kitchen paper.

Grease a shallow, heatproof dish with butter, then arrange the fish in it. Season with salt and pepper.

In a separate bowl, mix together the remaining butter with the garlic. Arrange pieces of the garlic butter all over the fish, then transfer to the grill. Cook for 7–8 minutes, turning once, until the fish is cooked through.

Remove the dish from the grill. Using a fish slice, remove the fillets from the dish and arrange on individual serving plates. Pour over the remaining melted butter from the dish, and garnish with sprigs of fresh parsley and strips of orange zest. Serve with crisp salad leaves and cherry tomato slices.

# oriental rainbow trout

| | |
|---|---|
| extremely easy | |
| serves 4 | |
| 10 minutes | |
| 5–6 minutes | |

### ingredients

4 rainbow trout fillets, about
  175 g/6 oz each
4 tbsp chilli oil
salt and pepper
2 tbsp lemon juice
1 garlic clove, finely chopped
1 tbsp finely grated fresh root ginger
1 tbsp freshly grated lemon grass
1 tbsp chopped fresh coriander

GARNISH
sprigs of fresh coriander
grated fresh coconut

freshly boiled rice, to serve

Preheat the grill to medium. Rinse the fish fillets under cold running water, then pat dry with kitchen paper.

Brush a shallow, heatproof dish with chilli oil, then arrange the fish in it. Season the fish with salt and pepper.

In a separate bowl, mix together the remaining oil with the lemon juice, garlic, ginger, lemon grass and coriander. Spread the mixture all over the fish, then transfer the dish to the grill. Cook for 5–6 minutes, turning once, or until the fish is cooked through.

Remove the dish from the grill. Using a fish slice, remove the fillets from the dish and arrange on individual serving plates. Pour over the remaining juices from the dish, garnish with coriander sprigs and grated coconut and serve with freshly boiled rice.

# barbecued swordfish

| | |
|---|---|
| very easy | |
| serves 4 | |
| 5 minutes + 1½ hours to marinate | |
| 8 minutes | |

## ingredients

4 swordfish steaks, about
150 g/5½ oz each
salt and pepper

MARINADE
3 tbsp rice wine or sherry
3 tbsp chilli oil
2 garlic cloves, finely chopped
juice of 1 lime
1 tbsp chopped fresh coriander

GARNISH
fresh coriander, finely chopped
slices of lime

TO SERVE
freshly cooked jacket potatoes
barbecued corn-on-the-cob
selection of fresh salad leaves

To make the marinade, put the rice wine, oil, garlic, lime juice and coriander into a bowl and mix together well.

Rinse the fish fillets under cold running water, then pat dry with kitchen paper. Arrange the fish in a shallow, non-metallic (glass or ceramic) dish, which will not react with acid. Season with salt and pepper, then pour over the marinade and turn the fish in the mixture until well coated. Cover with clingfilm and refrigerate for about 1½ hours.

When the fish is thoroughly marinated, lift it out of the marinade and barbecue over hot coals for about 4 minutes. Turn the fish over, brush with more marinade and barbecue on the other side for another 4 minutes, or until cooked through.

Remove from the heat and garnish with chopped fresh coriander and slices of lime. Serve with hot jacket potatoes, barbecued corn-on-the-cob and a selection of salad leaves.

# steamed sea bream with ginger

| | | **ingredients** | |
|---|---|---|---|
| easy | | 500 g/1 lb 2 oz sea bream or perch fillets | 1 tbsp finely grated lemon rind |
| | | 1 garlic clove, finely chopped | 1 tbsp finely grated fresh root ginger |
| serves 4 | | 1 small red chilli, deseeded and finely chopped | GARNISH |
| | | 2 tbsp Thai fish sauce (nam pla) | sprigs of fresh coriander |
| 15 minutes | | 3 tbsp lemon juice | wedges of lemon |
| | | 100 ml/3 ½ fl oz fish stock | TO SERVE |
| | | 3 spring onions, trimmed and finely sliced | freshly cooked egg noodles |
| 10 minutes | | | fresh bread rolls, optional |

Rinse the fish fillets under cold running water, then pat dry with kitchen paper. Make several fairly deep diagonal cuts into the fish on both sides. Put the fish on a heatproof plate that is slightly smaller than your wok. The plate should have a rim.

In a separate bowl, mix together the garlic, chilli, fish sauce, lemon juice and stock. Pour this mixture over the fish. Scatter over the spring onions, lemon rind and ginger.

Fill a large wok with boiling water up to a depth of about 4 cm/ 1 ½ inches. Bring it back to the boil, then set a rack or trivet inside the wok. Put the plate of fish on top of the rack, then cover the wok with a lid. Lower the heat a little and steam the fish for about 10 minutes, or until cooked through.

Lift out the fish and arrange on the freshly cooked egg noodles. Garnish with coriander sprigs and lemon wedges, and serve with fresh bread rolls (if using).

# salmon with brandy sauce

| | | **ingredients** | |
|---|---|---|---|
| very easy | 650 g/1 lb 7 oz salmon steaks<br>3 tbsp butter<br>1 garlic clove, finely chopped<br>1 onion, chopped<br>1 leek, trimmed and finely sliced<br>2 tbsp chopped fresh coriander<br>4 tbsp brandy<br>6 tbsp single cream<br>1 tbsp lime juice<br>salt and pepper | GARNISH<br>fresh coriander, chopped<br>Parmesan cheese, freshly grated<br>8 cherry tomatoes, halved and grilled<br><br>TO SERVE<br>freshly cooked tagliatelle<br>slices of fresh bread |
| serves 4 | | |
| 10 minutes | | |
| 25 minutes | | |

Rinse the fish steaks under cold running water, then pat dry with kitchen paper.

Melt 2 tablespoons of the butter in a large frying pan over a medium heat. Add the fish and cook for 3 minutes, then turn over and cook on the other side for a further 3 minutes. Using a fish slice, lift out the fish and keep it warm.

Melt the remaining butter in the frying pan over a medium heat, then add the garlic, onion and leek. Cook for 4 minutes until slightly softened, then stir in the coriander, brandy, cream and lime juice. Season with salt and pepper. Continue to cook, stirring, for 10–12 minutes.

Divide the tagliatelle between serving plates. Arrange the fish on top and pour over the sauce. Garnish with chopped fresh coriander, grated Parmesan and the grilled tomatoes. Serve with slices of fresh bread.

# mixed fish curry

| | |
|---|---|
| very easy | |
| serves 4 | |
| 10 minutes | |
| 25 minutes | |

### ingredients

3 tbsp butter
3 garlic cloves, chopped
2 shallots, chopped
1 red chilli, deseeded and chopped
4 tbsp grated coconut
pinch of cayenne pepper
1 tsp mild curry powder
½ tsp garam masala
350 ml/12 fl oz water
350 g/12 oz cod fillets
350 g/12 oz haddock fillets

1 tbsp orange juice
1 tbsp chopped fresh coriander
1 tbsp chopped fresh parsley
salt and pepper

GARNISH
fresh coriander, chopped
slices of orange

TO SERVE
freshly boiled rice
plain poppadoms

Melt the butter in a large frying pan over a low heat. Add the garlic and shallots and cook, stirring, for about 3 minutes until slightly softened. Add the chilli, coconut, cayenne pepper, curry powder and garam masala and cook for a further 2 minutes. Stir in the water and bring to the boil, then lower the heat and simmer for 7–8 minutes.

Rinse the fish under cold running water, then pat dry with kitchen paper. Add the fish to the pan with the orange juice and herbs, and season with salt and pepper. Simmer for another 7–8 minutes until the fish is cooked through.

Arrange the freshly boiled rice on serving plates, then spoon over the curry, dividing the fish fillets evenly between the plates. Garnish with chopped fresh coriander and orange slices. Serve at once with crispy plain poppadoms.

# fish kedgeree

| | |
|---|---|
| very easy | |
| serves 4 | |
| 10 minutes | |
| 30 minutes | |

## ingredients

3 tbsp butter
2 shallots, chopped
1 leek, trimmed and finely sliced
300 g/10½ oz brown rice
600 ml/1 pint fish stock
200 g/7 oz salmon fillets
200 g/7 oz smoked haddock fillets

300 ml/10 fl oz milk
½ tsp garam masala
salt and pepper

finely shredded Chinese lettuce leaves,
   to garnish

fresh bread rolls, to serve

Preheat the oven to 190°C/375°F/Gas Mark 5. Melt the butter in a large frying pan over a low heat. Add the shallots and leek and cook, stirring, for about 4 minutes until slightly softened. Add the rice, then stir in the stock and bring to the boil.

Transfer the shallot mixture to a large, ovenproof casserole dish. Cover and bake in the centre of the preheated oven for about 25 minutes, until all the liquid has been absorbed.

About 5 minutes before the end of the cooking time, rinse the fish fillets under cold running water, then pat dry with kitchen paper. Pour the milk into a saucepan and bring to the boil. Add the fish and poach for 5–6 minutes until tender.

Remove the rice from the oven. Drain the fish, discard the milk and flake the fillets into small pieces. Add the fish and garam masala to the rice, and season with salt and pepper. Stir together well and garnish with shredded Chinese lettuce leaves. Serve with bread rolls.

# mixed fish & potato pie

| | | ingredients | |
|---|---|---|---|
| | easy | 350 g/12 oz haddock fillets | 1 tbsp chopped fresh coriander |
| | | 350 g/12 oz halibut fillets | 2 onions, 1 grated and 1 sliced |
| | | 350 g/12 oz salmon fillets | salt and pepper |
| | serves 4 | 600 ml/1 pint milk | 75 g/3 oz Cheddar cheese, grated |
| | | 125 ml/4 fl oz brandy | |
| | | 1 kg/2 lb 4 oz potatoes, sliced | selection of freshly cooked vegetables, |
| | | 5 tbsp butter, plus extra for greasing |   to serve |
| | 15 minutes | 3 tbsp plain flour | |
| | | 1 tbsp chopped fresh parsley | |
| | 1 hour 10 minutes | | |

Preheat the oven to 200°C/400°F/Gas Mark 6. Rinse all the fish, then pat dry with kitchen paper. Pour the milk into a pan and bring to the boil. Add the haddock and halibut and cook gently for 10 minutes. Lift out and set aside. Reserve the milk. In a separate pan, cook the salmon in the brandy over a low heat for 10 minutes. Lift out and set aside. Reserve the cooking liquid. Cut all the fish into small chunks.

Cook the potatoes in a pan of lightly salted water for 15 minutes. Meanwhile, in another pan, melt the butter over a low heat, stir in the flour and cook for 1 minute. Stir in the reserved milk and brandy liquid to make a smooth sauce. Bring to the boil then simmer for 10 minutes. Remove from the heat and stir in the herbs. Drain and mash the potatoes, then add the grated onion. Season. Grease a large pie dish with butter then add the fish. Top with sliced onion. Pour over enough sauce to cover. Top with mashed potato, then grated cheese. Bake for 30 minutes. Serve with cooked vegetables.

# cod puff pie

| | | ingredients | |
|---|---|---|---|
| easy | | | |
| serves 4 | 700 g/1 lb 9 oz cod fillets | 2 tbsp chopped fresh basil | |
| | 600 ml/1 pint fish stock | 1 tbsp sherry | |
| | 250 g/9 oz potatoes, sliced | plain flour, for dusting | |
| | 2 tbsp butter | 1 packet frozen puff pastry dough, | |
| | 1 onion, sliced | defrosted | |
| | 1 garlic clove, chopped | salt and pepper | |
| 20 minutes | 1 carrot, sliced | 1 tbsp milk | |
| | 2 celery sticks, trimmed and sliced | | |
| | 100 g/3½ oz chestnut mushrooms, | TO SERVE | |
| 1 hour | wiped and sliced | crisp lettuce leaves | |
| | 4 tomatoes, sliced | freshly cooked mangetouts | |

Rinse the cod and pat dry. Bring the stock to the boil, add the cod and simmer for 10 minutes. Drain; cut into chunks. Meanwhile, cook the potatoes in salted water for 5 minutes. Drain. Melt half the butter in a frying pan over a low heat. Add the onion and garlic; cook for 3 minutes. Add the carrot and celery; cook for 5 minutes. Lift out the vegetables; set aside. Preheat the oven to 200°C/400°F/Gas Mark 6.

Melt the remaining butter in the frying pan. Add the mushrooms and tomatoes and cook for 7 minutes. Stir in the basil and sherry. Cook for 1 minute. On a floured surface, roll out enough dough to line a large pie dish, with an overhang of 2.5 cm/1 inch. Put some tomato mixture into the lined dish. Top with a layer of cod, then a vegetable layer, then a potato layer. Repeat the layers to fill the pie. Season. Top with pastry, trim and crimp, and make a slit in the top. Decorate with dough fish shapes; brush with milk. Bake for 30 minutes. Serve with crisp lettuce leaves and freshly cooked mangetouts.

# haddock cobbler

| | | ingredients | |
|---|---|---|---|
| easy | | 350 g/12 oz cod fillets | PASTRY |
| | | 350 g/12 oz haddock fillets | 4 tbsp butter |
| serves 4 | | 500 ml/18 fl oz milk | 140 g/5 oz plain flour |
| | | 1 bay leaf | 1 tsp baking powder |
| | | 4 tbsp butter | pinch of nutmeg |
| | | 6 tbsp plain flour | 1 egg yolk |
| 25 minutes | | 1 tbsp chopped fresh dill | 4 tbsp milk |
| | | 1 tbsp chopped fresh parsley | |
| | | 200 g/7 oz Cheddar cheese, grated | TO SERVE |
| 50 minutes | | salt and pepper | cherry tomatoes, halved |
| | | | freshly cooked green beans |

Rinse the fish and pat dry. Pour the milk into a large pan, add the bay leaf and bring to the boil. Lower the heat, add the fish and cook gently for 10 minutes. Lift out the fish and set aside. Discard the bay leaf. Reserve the milk. Melt the butter in a pan. Stir in the flour; cook gently for 1 minute. Gradually stir in enough reserved milk to make a smooth sauce. Bring to the boil, then simmer for 5 minutes. Remove from the heat, stir in the herbs and half the cheese. Season. Preheat the oven to 200°C/400°F/Gas Mark 6. Cut the fish into chunks.

In a separate bowl, rub the butter into the flour, then add the baking powder and nutmeg. Stir in the egg yolk and enough milk to make a pliable dough. Roll out to 1 cm/½ inch thick. Using a pastry cutter, cut out rounds about 5–7.5 cm/2–3 inches in diameter. Put the fish chunks into a pie dish. Pour over the sauce and top with the pastry rounds. Sprinkle over the remaining cheese. Bake for 30 minutes. Serve with halved cherry tomatoes and freshly cooked green beans.

# baked dover sole
# with vegetables

| | |
|---|---|
| very easy | |
| serves 4 | |
| 10 minutes | |
| 50 minutes | |

### ingredients

4 Dover sole fillets, about
650 g/1 lb 7 oz each
3 tbsp extra-virgin olive oil
3 shallots, chopped
1 garlic clove, chopped
1 courgette, sliced
2 spring onions, trimmed and chopped
425 g/15 oz canned plum tomatoes
6 black olives, stoned and sliced

6 green olives, stoned and sliced
2 tbsp chopped fresh basil
salt and pepper
6 tbsp freshly grated Parmesan

black and green olives, stoned,
to garnish

selection of freshly cooked vegetables,
to serve

Preheat the oven to 190°C/375°F/Gas Mark 5. Rinse the fish fillets under cold running water and pat dry with kitchen paper.

Heat 2 tablespoons of the oil in a large frying pan over a low heat. Add the shallots and garlic and cook, stirring, for about 3 minutes until slightly softened. Add the courgette and spring onions and cook for another 4 minutes, stirring. Add the tomatoes and their juice, along with the olives and basil. Season with salt and pepper and simmer for another 10 minutes.

Brush a shallow, ovenproof baking dish with the remaining oil, then arrange the fish fillets in it. Remove the pan from the heat and pour the sauce over the fish. Sprinkle over the Parmesan and bake in the centre of the preheated oven for about 30 minutes, or until the fish is cooked through.

Remove from the oven and transfer to serving plates. Garnish with black and green olives and serve with freshly cooked vegetables.

# mediterranean-style sea bass

| | | **ingredients** | |
|---|---|---|---|
| | extremely easy | 4 tbsp basil-flavoured oil or extra-virgin olive oil | GARNISH wedges of lemon |
| | serves 4 | 750 g/1 lb 10 oz sea bass fillets | sprigs of fresh basil |
| | | 12 black olives, stoned and quartered | |
| | | 1 tbsp lemon juice | fresh red and green salad leaves, to serve |
| | 5 minutes | 2 tbsp dry white wine | |
| | | 2 tbsp chopped fresh basil | |
| | | salt and pepper | |
| | 8–10 minutes | | |

Heat the oil in a large frying pan over a medium heat. Put the fish fillets into the pan and cook for 5 minutes, turning once, or until cooked through.

Add the olives, lemon juice, wine and basil to the pan, and season with salt and pepper. Cook for a further 2 minutes, stirring.

Arrange the red and green salad leaves on serving plates. Remove the pan from the heat and use a fish slice to lift out the fish and place it on top of the salad leaves. Pour over any remaining juices from the pan, garnish with lemon wedges and sprigs of fresh basil and serve.

# roasted salmon
# with lemon & herbs

| | |
|---|---|
| very easy | |
| serves 4 | |
| 10 minutes | |
| 15 minutes | |

## ingredients

6 tbsp extra-virgin olive oil
1 onion, sliced
1 leek, trimmed and sliced
juice of ½ lemon
2 tbsp chopped fresh parsley
2 tbsp chopped fresh dill
salt and pepper
500 g/1 lb 2 oz salmon fillets

GARNISH
slices of lemon
sprigs of fresh dill

freshly cooked baby spinach leaves,
  to serve

Preheat the oven to 200°C/400°F/Gas Mark 6. Heat 1 tablespoon of the oil in a frying pan over a medium heat. Add the onion and leek and cook, stirring, for about 4 minutes until slightly softened.

Meanwhile, put the remaining oil in a small bowl with the lemon juice and herbs, and season. Stir together well. Rinse the fish under cold running water, then pat dry with kitchen paper. Arrange the fish in a shallow, ovenproof baking dish.

Remove the frying pan from the heat and spread the onion and leek over the fish. Pour the oil mixture over the top, ensuring that everything is well coated. Roast in the centre of the preheated oven for about 10 minutes or until the fish is cooked through.

Arrange the cooked spinach on serving plates. Remove the fish and vegetables from the oven and arrange on top of the spinach. Garnish with lemon slices and sprigs of dill. Serve at once.

# roasted mackerel
# mediterranean-style

| | |
|---|---|
| very easy | |
| serves 4 | |
| 15 minutes | |
| 25 minutes | |

### ingredients

4 tbsp basil oil or extra-virgin olive oil
2 garlic cloves, chopped
1 onion, sliced
2 courgettes, trimmed and sliced
6 plum tomatoes, sliced
12 black olives, stoned and halved
1 tbsp tomato purée
4 tbsp red wine
100 ml/3½ fl oz fish stock
2 tbsp chopped fresh parsley

2 tbsp chopped fresh basil
salt and pepper
4 large mackerel, cleaned

GARNISH
slices of lemon
sprigs of fresh basil

TO SERVE
freshly cooked spaghetti
fresh salad leaves and spring onions

Preheat the oven to 200°C/400°F/Gas Mark 6. Heat 1 tablespoon of the oil in a large frying pan over a medium heat. Add the garlic, onion and courgettes and cook, stirring, for about 4 minutes.

Add the tomatoes, olives, tomato purée, wine, stock and herbs. Season with salt and pepper and bring to the boil. Lower the heat to medium and cook, stirring, for 10 minutes.

Rinse the fish under cold running water, then pat dry with kitchen paper. Arrange the fish in a shallow, ovenproof baking dish, then remove the frying pan from the heat and spread the tomato sauce over the fish. Roast in the centre of the preheated oven for about 10 minutes or until the fish is cooked through.

Remove from the oven, arrange the fish in its sauce on plates of freshly cooked spaghetti, and garnish with lemon slices and sprigs of basil. Serve accompanied by a side salad of fresh salad leaves and spring onions.

# prawn & haddock curry

| | | **ingredients** | |
|---|---|---|---|
| very easy | | 2 tbsp vegetable oil | 125 ml/4 fl oz fish stock |
| | | 2 garlic cloves, chopped | 450 g/1 lb haddock fillets, skinned |
| serves 4 | | 4 shallots, chopped | 350 g/12 oz prawns, peeled and |
| | | 1 tbsp grated fresh root ginger | deveined |
| | | 1 tsp mild curry powder | 5 tbsp natural yogurt |
| | | 1 red pepper, deseeded and chopped | salt and pepper |
| 15 minutes | | 200 g/7 oz canned red kidney beans, | |
| | | drained | fresh coconut, grated, to garnish |
| | | 3 tomatoes, chopped | TO SERVE |
| 25 minutes | | 3 tbsp grated fresh coconut | freshly boiled rice |
| | | 3 tbsp chopped fresh coriander | naan bread |

Heat the oil in a large saucepan over a low heat. Add the garlic, shallots, ginger and curry powder and cook, stirring, for about 4 minutes until the shallots have softened slightly.

Add the red pepper, kidney beans, tomatoes, coconut and coriander. Stir in the stock. Season with salt and pepper and bring to the boil. Lower the heat and simmer, stirring occasionally, for 15 minutes.

Rinse the fish fillets under cold running water, then pat dry with kitchen paper. Cut the fish into small chunks, then add it to the pan. Cook for 2 minutes. Add the prawns and cook for a further 3 minutes, or until all the fish is cooked through, but do not overcook.

Remove from the heat and stir in the yogurt. Arrange the fish curry on plates of freshly boiled rice. Garnish with grated coconut and serve with naan bread.

# seafood gratin

| | |
|---|---|
| easy | |
| serves 4 | |
| 15 minutes | |
| 1 hour | |

## ingredients

450 g/1 lb cod fillets
225 g/8 oz prawns, peeled and
  deveined
225 g/8 oz scallops
3 tbsp extra-virgin olive oil
1 garlic clove, chopped
4 spring onions, trimmed and chopped
1 courgette, sliced
425 g/15 oz canned plum tomatoes

2 tbsp chopped fresh basil
salt and pepper
50 g/1¾ oz fresh breadcrumbs
75 g/2¾ oz Cheddar cheese, grated

freshly cooked broccoli and cauliflower,
  to serve

Bring a large pan of water to the boil, then lower the heat to medium. Rinse the cod, pat dry with kitchen paper and add to the pan. Cook for 5 minutes. Add the prawns and cook for 3 minutes, then add the scallops and cook for 2 minutes. Drain, refresh under cold running water and drain again. Preheat the oven to 190°C/375°F/Gas Mark 5.

Heat 2 tablespoons of the oil in a frying pan over a low heat. Add the garlic and spring onions and cook, stirring, for 3 minutes. Add the courgette and cook for 3 minutes, then add the tomatoes and their juice, and the basil. Season and simmer for 10 minutes.

Brush a shallow baking dish with the remaining oil and arrange the seafood in it. Remove the pan from the heat and pour the sauce over the fish. Scatter over the breadcrumbs and top with cheese. Bake for 30 minutes until golden. Remove from the oven and serve with freshly cooked broccoli and cauliflower.

# index